YOU DO YOU

ICE HOUSE BOOKS

Published by Ice House Books

Compiled by Zulekhá Afzal
Designed and illustrated by Emily Curtis

Ice House Books is an imprint of Half Moon Bay Limited
The Ice House, 124 Walcot Street, Bath, BA1 5BG
www.icehousebooks.co.uk

We have updated some older quotes with generic pronouns, shown in square brackets, as the meaning of these quotes are relevant to everybody.

ISBN 978-1-912867-89-9

Printed in China

TO:

FROM:

DON'T CHANGE
WHO YOU ARE
FOR ANYONE.

BE YOURSELF:
EVERYONE ELSE
IS ALREADY
TAKEN.

OSCAR WILDE

By being yourself, you put something wonderful in the world that was not there before.

EDWIN ELLIOT

YOU SAY
I'M DIFFERENT...
I SAY,
HELL YEAH I AM!

STAY TRUE TO YOURSELF AND WHAT MAKES YOU SMILE.

TO BE YOURSELF IN
A WORLD THAT IS
CONSTANTLY TRYING
TO MAKE YOU
SOMETHING ELSE
IS THE GREATEST
ACCOMPLISHMENT.

RALPH WALDO EMERSON

WHEN YOU ARE
CONTENT TO BE
SIMPLY YOURSELF
AND DON'T COMPARE
OR COMPETE,
EVERYONE WILL
RESPECT YOU.

LAO TZU

Reflect your light for everyone to see.

IT IS NEVER TOO LATE TO BE WHAT YOU MIGHT HAVE BEEN.

GEORGE ELIOT

SOMETIMES THE MOST IMPORTANT THING IN A WHOLE DAY IS THE REST WE TAKE BETWEEN TWO DEEP BREATHS.

ETTY HILLESUM

No one knows
how to do you
like you do.

NEVER VIOLATE
THE SACREDNESS
OF YOUR
INDIVIDUAL
SELF-RESPECT.

THEODORE PARKER

BE WHO YOU WERE CREATED TO BE, AND YOU WILL SET THE WORLD ON FIRE.

ST. CATHERINE OF SIENA

TRUST YOUR JOURNEY.

I DON'T WANT
EVERYONE TO
LIKE ME; I SHOULD
THINK LESS OF
MYSELF IF SOME
PEOPLE DID.

HENRY JAMES

The life of every [person] is a diary in which [they] mean to write one story, and write another.

J. M. BARRIE

THE INDIVIDUAL HAS ALWAYS HAD TO STRUGGLE TO KEEP FROM BEING OVERWHELMED BY THE TRIBE. IF YOU TRY IT, YOU WILL BE LONELY OFTEN, AND SOMETIMES FRIGHTENED. BUT NO PRICE IS TOO HIGH TO PAY FOR THE PRIVILEGE OF OWNING YOURSELF.

RUDYARD KIPLING

DIFFERENT ISN'T DIFFERENT IF YOU'RE TRYING TO BE LIKE EVERYONE ELSE.

IT TAKES COURAGE TO STAY TRUE TO WHO YOU ARE.

You yourself, as much as anybody in the entire universe, deserve your love and affection.

BUDDHA

BE YOURSELF, BUT ALWAYS YOUR BETTER SELF.

KARL G. MAESER

DON'T FORGET
TO TELL
YOURSELF
YOU'RE GREAT.

BELIEVE IN
THE POWER
OF YOU.

[Those] who live in harmony with [themselves] live in harmony with the universe.

MARCUS AURELIUS

DO NOT FEAR
TO BE ECCENTRIC
IN OPINION,
FOR EVERY OPINION
NOW ACCEPTED WAS
ONCE ECCENTRIC.

BERTRAND RUSSELL

YOU HAVE THE POTENTIAL TO DO ANYTHING.

EQUALITY
LOVES
INDIVUALITY.

I am no bird;
and no net
ensnares me:
I am a free
being with an
independent will.

CHARLOTTE BRONTË,
JANE EYRE

THE WORST LONELINESS IS TO NOT BE COMFORTABLE WITH YOURSELF.

MARK TWAIN

THIS ABOVE ALL:
TO THINE OWN
SELF BE TRUE.

WILLIAM SHAKESPEARE,
HAMLET

RESPECT YOURSELF AND OTHERS WILL RESPECT YOU.

CONFUCIUS

You are unique.
Own it.

DON'T LET ANYONE PUT A MOUNTAIN IN YOUR WAY.

THE DEEPEST PRINCIPLE IN HUMAN NATURE IS THE CRAVING TO BE APPRECIATED.

WILLIAM JAMES

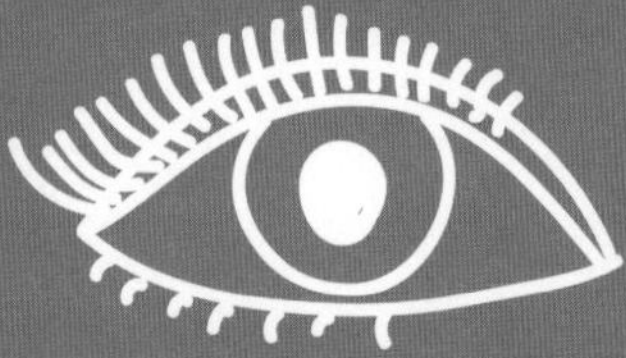

ORIGINALITY IS SIMPLY A PAIR OF FRESH EYES.

THOMAS W. HIGGINSON

You are
the best version
of yourself.

TRANSFORM
THE NORM.

OH, NEVER MIND
THE FASHION.
WHEN ONE HAS A
STYLE OF ONE'S OWN,
IT IS ALWAYS
20 TIMES BETTER.

MARGARET OLIPHANT

FOLLOW YOUR OWN STAR.

DANTE ALIGHIERI

Do more of what makes you happy.

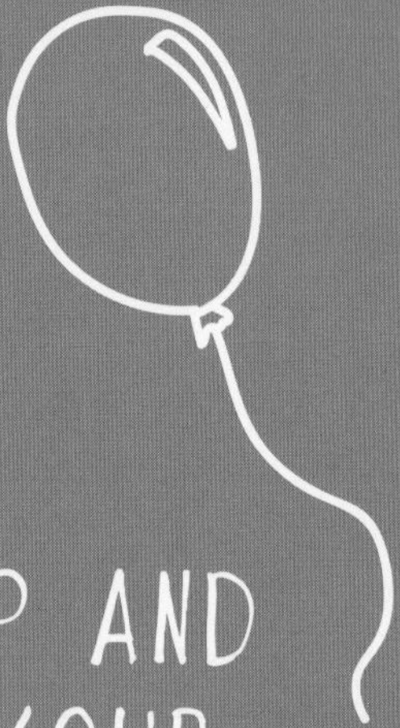

JUMP UP AND
GRAB YOUR
DREAMS.

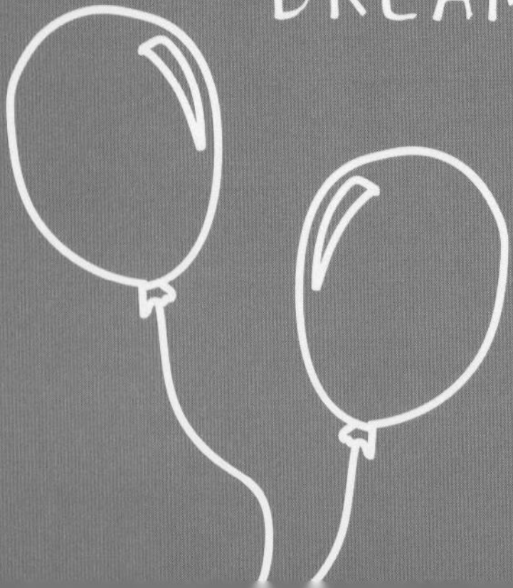

WITH CONFIDENCE, YOU HAVE WON BEFORE YOU HAVE STARTED.

MARCUS GARVEY

Don't think, just do.

HORACE

YOU WILL NEVER INFLUENCE THE WORLD BY TRYING TO BE LIKE IT.

I'M NOT EXACTLY LIKE YOU BUT I'M NOT COMPLETELY DIFFERENT, EITHER.

I PREFER TO BE TRUE
TO MYSELF, EVEN
AT THE HAZARD
OF INCURRING THE
RIDICULE OF OTHERS,
RATHER THAN TO BE
FALSE, AND TO INCUR
MY OWN ABHORRENCE.

FREDERICK DOUGLASS

Learn to be what you are, and learn to resign with a good grace all that you are not.

HENRI-FRÉDÉRIC AMIEL

SELF-LOVE IS
THE GREATEST
MIDDLE FINGER
OF ALL TIME.

FOCUS ON WHAT
MAKES YOU HAPPY,
INSTEAD OF WHAT
YOU THINK WILL
MAKE EVERYONE
ELSE HAPPY.

BE WHAT YOU ARE.
THIS IS THE
FIRST STEP
TOWARD BECOMING
BETTER THAN
YOU ARE.

JULIUS CHARLES HARE

TRUE ORIGINALITY CONSISTS NOT IN A NEW MANNER BUT IN A NEW VISION.

EDITH WHARTON

Be congruent.
Be authentic.
Be your true self.

MAHATMA GANDHI

IT IS BETTER
TO FAIL IN
ORIGINALITY
THAN TO SUCCEED
IN IMITATION.

HERMAN MELVILLE

HUM ALONG
TO YOUR
OWN SONG.

DON'T BE AFRAID
TO DREAM BIG
AND FLY HIGH.

Create your own method. Don't depend slavishly on mine. Make up something that will work for you! But keep breaking traditions, I beg you.

KONSTANTIN STANISLAVSKI

NO ONE EVER MADE
A DIFFERENCE
BY BEING LIKE
EVERYONE ELSE.

P. T. BARNUM

CHASE WHAT MAKES YOU SMILE AND LAUGH.

DON'T LET FOMO STOP YOU FROM TAKING A MOMENT TO YOURSELF. FOMO CAN EASILY TURN INTO JOMO.

One life is all we have and we live it as we believe in living it. But to sacrifice what you are and to live without belief, that is a fate more terrible than dying.

JOAN OF ARC

LET YOURSELF BE DRAWN BY THE STRONGER PULL OF THAT WHICH YOU TRULY LOVE.

RUMI

STOP COMPARING YOURSELF TO OTHER PEOPLE AND THEIR IDEALS.

Don't try to be a doughnut when you're a cupcake.

THERE IS ONLY ONE WAY TO HAPPINESS AND THAT IS TO CEASE WORRYING ABOUT THINGS WHICH ARE BEYOND THE POWER OF OUR WILL.

EPICTETUS

HATEFUL TO ME AS
THE GATES OF HADES
IS THAT [PERSON]
WHO HIDES ONE THING
IN [THEIR] HEART AND
SPEAKS ANOTHER.

HOMER

LOVING YOURSELF IS THE GREATEST REVOLUTION.

WAKE UP.
KICK ASS.
REPEAT.

You are the only person on earth who can use your ability.

ZIG ZIGLAR

AS IS OUR CONFIDENCE, SO IS OUR CAPACITY.

WILLIAM HAZLITT

BE YOUR OWN CHEERLEADER.

IF ONE ADVANCES CONFIDENTLY IN THE DIRECTION OF [THEIR] DREAMS, AND ENDEAVOURS TO LIVE THE LIFE WHICH [THEY] HAVE IMAGINED, [THEY] WILL MEET WITH A SUCCESS UNEXPECTED IN COMMON HOURS.

HENRY DAVID THOREAU

To love oneself is the beginning of a lifelong romance.

OSCAR WILDE

EMBRACE YOUR SUPERPOWERS.

ORIGINALITY DOES NOT CONSIST IN SAYING WHAT NO ONE HAS EVER SAID BEFORE, BUT IN SAYING EXACTLY WHAT YOU THINK YOURSELF.

JAMES STEPHENS

I AM NOT AFRAID OF STORMS FOR I AM LEARNING HOW TO SAIL MY SHIP.

LOUISA MAY ALCOTT

You are fabulous.
Don't ever forget that.

BELIEVE IN YOURSELF AND YOU'LL BE UNSTOPPABLE.

THEY CAN DO ALL BECAUSE THEY THINK THEY CAN.

VIRGIL

BELIEVE YOU
CAN AND
YOU'RE
HALFWAY
THERE.

THEODORE ROOSEVELT

Be the flower
in a field
of grass.

I WISH I COULD SHOW YOU, WHEN YOU ARE LONELY OR IN DARKNESS, THE ASTONISHING LIGHT OF YOUR OWN BEING.

HAFIZ OF SHIRAZ

BLAME IT OR
PRAISE IT,
THERE IS NO
DENYING
THE WILD
HORSE IN US.

VIRGINIA WOOLF

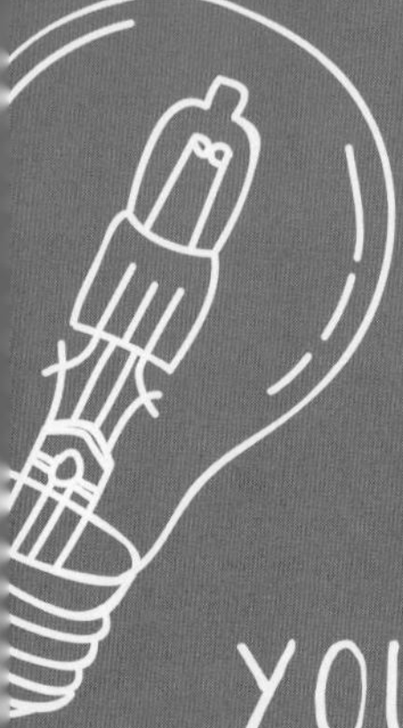

YOU ARE YOUR OWN GUIDING LIGHT.

One person with passion is better than forty people merely interested.

E. M. FORSTER

BIG SHOTS
ARE ONLY
LITTLE SHOTS
WHO KEPT
SHOOTING.

CHRISTOPHER MORLEY

DON'T FORGET TO TAKE TIME OUT FOR YOURSELF.

WHERE WOULD
THE FUN BE IF WE
WERE ALL BORN
THE SAME?

I celebrate myself,
and sing myself.

WALT WHITMAN

I AM OUT WITH LANTERNS, LOOKING FOR MYSELF.

EMILY DICKINSON

APPRECIATE
THE BEAUTY
INSIDE YOU.

Write your own story.

INSIST UPON YOURSELF. BE ORIGINAL.

RALPH WALDO EMERSON

MY DEAR,
I DON'T GIVE
A DAMN.

MARGARET MITCHELL,
GONE WITH THE WIND

DON'T SPEND ALL
YOUR TIME TRYING
TO BE WHAT OTHER
PEOPLE WANT.

FIND YOURSELF
AND BE THAT
PERSON INSTEAD.

ALWAYS LOOK
FOR THE
BEAUTY IN
OTHER PEOPLES'
DIFFERENCES.

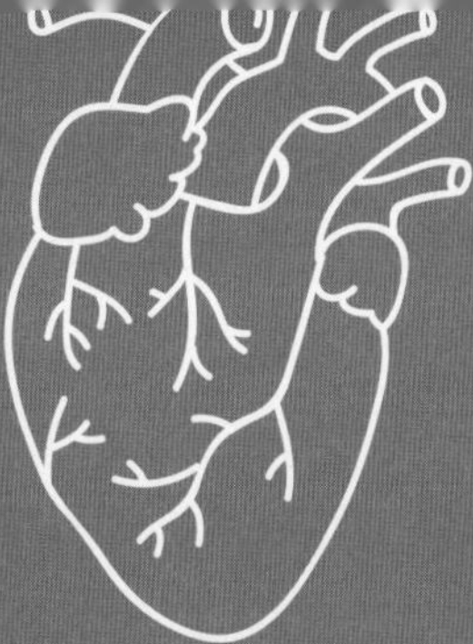

Wherever you go,
go with all
your heart.

CONFUCIUS

LEND YOURSELF
TO OTHERS, BUT
GIVE YOURSELF
TO YOURSELF.

MICHEL DE MONTAIGNE

WE ARE
ENRICHED BY
OUR RECIPROCATE
DIFFERENCES.

PAUL VALÉRY

DON'T DENY YOUR
INNER UNICORN.

What we think, we become.

BUDDHA

SELF-LOVE,
MY LIEGE, IS NOT
SO VILE A SIN,
AS SELF-NEGLECTING.

WILLIAM SHAKESPEARE,
HENRY V

TAKE ME AS
I AM OR
NOT AT ALL.

The most significant relationship you'll have is with yourself, so remember to be kind to yourself.

THE SECRET OF HAPPINESS IS NOT IN DOING WHAT ONE LIKES, BUT IN LIKING WHAT ONE DOES.

J. M. BARRIE

CARE ABOUT
WHAT OTHER
PEOPLE THINK
AND YOU WILL
ALWAYS BE
THEIR PRISONER.

LAO TZU

TRUST YOURSELF.

BE
YOUR
WILD
SELF.

Tension is who you think you should be, relaxation is who you are.

CHINESE PROVERB

LIFE ISN'T
ABOUT FINDING
YOURSELF.
LIFE IS ABOUT
CREATING
YOURSELF.

GEORGE BERNARD SHAW

DON'T DOUBT YOURSELF OR YOUR DREAMS.

NEVER GIVE
UP ON WHAT
MAKES YOU, YOU.

Best be yourself, imperial, plain and true.

ROBERT BROWNING

I AM MYSELF,
AND YOU ARE YOU.
BLESSED BE THE DAY
THAT WE ACCEPT THAT.

MURIEL STRODE

TAKE CARE
OF YOURSELF
AND YOU'LL BE
ABLE TO CARE
FOR OTHERS.

GIVE YOURSELF
THE SPACE
TO BREATHE.

Man conquers the world by conquering himself.

ZENO OF CITIUM

A [PERSON] CANNOT BE COMFORTABLE WITHOUT [THEIR] OWN APPROVAL.

MARK TWAIN

YOUR DIFFERENCES
ARE A GIFT.

Absorb each moment but know when it's time to let some of them go.

WE ARE ALL BORN ORIGINALS.

EDWARD YOUNG

WHY SHOULD WE WORRY ABOUT WHAT OTHERS THINK OF US, DO WE HAVE MORE CONFIDENCE IN THEIR OPINIONS THAN WE DO OUR OWN?

BRIGHAM YOUNG

DON'T SHY AWAY FROM YOUR AUTHENTIC SELF.

THE WORLD
NEEDS YOU.

He who trims himself to suit everyone will soon whittle himself away.

RAYMOND HULL

WHEN YOU DOUBT YOUR POWER, YOU GIVE POWER TO YOUR DOUBT.

HONORÉ DE BALZAC

IT AIN'T WHAT THEY CALL YOU, IT'S WHAT YOU ANSWER TO.

W. C. FIELDS

Love your journey.

ACT AS IF WHAT YOU DO MAKES A DIFFERENCE. IT DOES.

WILLIAM JAMES

WE ARE SO ACCUSTOMED TO DISGUISE OURSELVES TO OTHERS THAT IN THE END WE BECOME DISGUISED TO OURSELVES.

FRANÇOIS DE LA ROCHEFOUCAULD

BEING YOU
IS WHAT
MAKES YOU
SPECIAL.

SELF-LOVE
ISN'T
SELFISH.

I will not let anyone walk through my mind with their dirty feet.

MAHATMA GANDHI

THERE IS JUST ONE LIFE FOR EACH OF US: OUR OWN.

EURIPIDES

SHINE BRIGHT
LIKE THE SUN.

Believing in yourself is the first secret to success.

IN THE END, IT'S NOT THE YEARS IN YOUR LIFE THAT COUNT. IT'S THE LIFE IN YOUR YEARS.

ABRAHAM LINCOLN

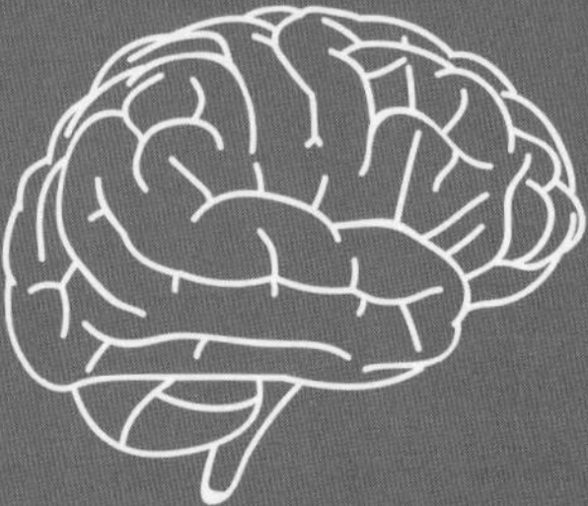

RULE YOUR MIND OR IT WILL RULE YOU.

HORACE

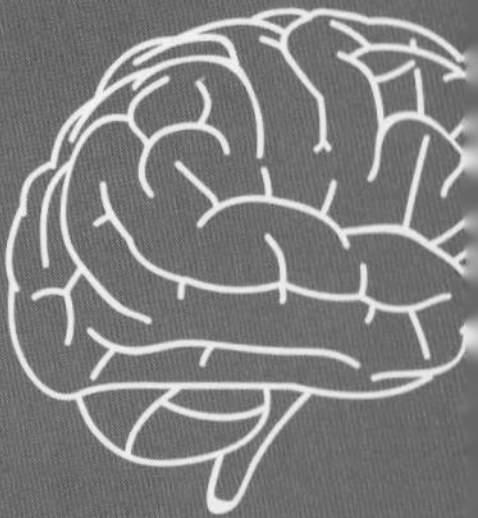

AS SOON AS YOU TRUST YOURSELF, YOU WILL KNOW HOW TO LIVE.

JOHANN WOLFGANG VON GOETHE

IT'S OKAY TO PRESS PAUSE.

Don't be satisfied with stories, how things have gone with others. Unfold your own myth.

RUMI

WE ARE BETRAYED BY WHAT IS FALSE WITHIN.

GEORGE MEREDITH

DON'T LET
ANYONE DULL
YOUR LIGHT.

YOU WERE BORN
TO BE UNIQUE.

*One day,
in retrospect,
the years of
struggle will
strike you as the
most beautiful.*

SIGMUND FREUD

IT IS THE
CHIEFEST POINT
OF HAPPINESS
THAT A [PERSON]
IS WILLING TO BE
WHAT [THEY ARE].

DESIDERIUS ERASMUS

TO LOVE
YOURSELF IS
TO UNDERSTAND
YOU DON'T NEED
TO BE PERFECT
TO BE GOOD.

F.L.Y
First Love
Yourself

FIND ECSTASY
IN LIFE; THE
MERE SENSE
OF LIVING IS
JOY ENOUGH.

EMILY DICKINSON

GO CONFIDENTLY
IN THE DIRECTION
OF YOUR DREAMS.
LIVE THE LIFE
YOU'VE IMAGINED.

HENRY DAVID THOREAU

Encourage yourself the way you encourage others.

You have the strength to ride out the storm.

PUT ALL EXCUSES ASIDE AND REMEMBER THIS: YOU ARE CAPABLE.

ZIG ZIGLAR

BEGIN AT
ONCE TO LIVE,
AND COUNT
EACH SEPARATE
DAY AS A
SEPARATE LIFE.

SENECA

REMEMBER
TO GIVE
SOME OF YOUR
LOVE TO
YOURSELF.

Be kind to yourself.

DO ANYTHING,
BUT LET IT
PRODUCE JOY.

HENRY MILLER

TO BE BEAUTIFUL
MEANS TO
BE YOURSELF.
YOU DON'T NEED
TO BE ACCEPTED
BY OTHERS.
YOU NEED TO
ACCEPT YOURSELF.

THICH NHAT HANH